Catalogue Of The Classical Antiquities From The Collection Of The Late Sir Gardner Wilkinson, Harrow School Museum

HARROW SCHOOL MUSEUM.

CATALOGUE

OF THE

CLASSICAL ANTIQUITIES

FROM THE COLLECTION OF THE LATE

SIR GARDNER WILKINSON.

BY

CECIL TORR, M.A.

Harrow

J. C. WILBEE

BOOKSELLER TO HARROW SCHOOL.

1887

CATALOGUE

OF THE

CLASSICAL ANTIQUITIES

FROM THE COLLECTION OF THE LATE

SIR GARDNER WILKINSON.

BY

CECIL TORR, M.A.

𝕳arrow

J. C. WILBEE

BOOKSELLER TO HARROW SCHOOL.

1887

Cambridge:

PRINTED BY C. J. CLAY, M.A. AND SONS

AT THE UNIVERSITY PRESS.

PREFACE.

SIR JOHN GARDNER WILKINSON transferred to the Governors
of Harrow School, partly by gift in his lifetime and partly by
bequest on his death, certain collections "upon condition that
the same be placed as soon as possible in a suitable and
convenient place at Harrow belonging to the said Governors
of Harrow School and that they be accessible to the Boys of
the said Harrow School and that they be not sold nor dispersed
nor removed thence." These collections comprised; firstly,
Egyptian antiquities; secondly, Classical antiquities; thirdly,
coins and medals; and fourthly, fossils and stones from
Derbyshire. They were placed in the Vaughan Library at
Harrow and remained there until last autumn, when they
were removed to the Museum lately erected at Harrow by the
Governors of the School.

Sir Gardner had been greatly interested, when an under-
graduate at Oxford, by the collections belonging to the
University; and he believed that he would have been equally
interested, when a boy at Harrow, by similar collections, had
such then belonged to the School. He was thus led to
transfer his own collections to the School, that in the future
any of the boys with the like tastes might, if they so pleased,
examine for themselves objects of Antiquity and of Art and
of Science. And it was his hope that other men, who had
been at Harrow as boys, would make similar contributions,
and that his own would be merely the nucleus of much more
extensive and varied collections.

The Egyptian and Classical antiquities thus transferred to
the School constitute in themselves two important collections,

which could not be formed afresh without the expenditure of much time and trouble and of £2500 at the least: but they do not in any sense constitute complete collections. It is therefore greatly to be desired that other men may follow Sir Gardner's example by gift or bequest of antiquities already in their possession or of sums of money for the purchase, as opportunity arises, of such antiquities as may most be needed.

Elaborate manuscript catalogues of the Egyptian and Classical antiquities were drawn up by Sir Gardner soon after 1864 when he made his first gift to Harrow. These contain verbal descriptions and coloured drawings of all the antiquities and long notes on many of them: and they will always possess a certain interest of their own. But in the last twenty years the study of antiquities has made marvellous progress: great masses of new facts have been ascertained; and very many accepted theories have consequently been abandoned or modified, while new theories have been formed. It therefore seemed desirable that the printed catalogues should be entirely independent works.

These printed catalogues of the Egyptian and Classical antiquities have been drawn up by Mr Wallis Budge and Mr Cecil Torr respectively, and have been printed at Mr Torr's expense. And thus some account of these important collections has at length been placed within reach of the boys of the School and of the public generally. The list of Kings appended to the Egyptian Catalogue will at the same time be of service to all students of Egyptology.

Last year the attention of the Governors of the School was directed by Mr Torr to the scandalously neglected condition in which Sir Gardner's collections then were: and a sum of money, which they very promptly voted, has since been expended under Mr Budge's direction in reorganizing the Egyptian collection. The Classical collection still needs reorganization.

CLASSICAL ANTIQUITIES.

WHEN Classical Learning was revived in Western Europe four centuries ago, its scope was the knowledge of the whole of the literature of ancient Greece and Rome, and of the civilization of which that literature was a product. It was then the chosen study of men of culture. Unhappily, it subsequently became the enforced study of youth of every sort: and its scope has been steadily contracted until in modern education, which aims at the training of the mind rather than at the acquisition of knowledge, it embraces only those small portions of the subject which have proved service-able in such training. The result is that, while it may be hoped that the results of this training are brilliant, it is certainly notorious that in this country any wide knowledge of that ancient civilization and its literature is altogether exceptional and that even a decent knowledge of its languages is not very common. Yet if one will study Latin and Greek simply as languages and the Classics simply as literature, it is surprisingly easy to acquire the power of reading Greek and Latin authors with rapidity and precision. And this power is the more worth acquiring, as it is the only outcome of a Classical education (apart from the unrivalled training above mentioned) by which a man is likely to set much store, when he is past five and twenty. There are plenty of readable books more or less neglected among the Classics themselves, Lucian and Pausanias and Athenæus, for example, in three very different styles: and if one cares to pass beyond the limits of the Classics, it is a relief to turn from the works which Roman poets and historians were content to fashion after Greek models, to the legal writings in which the best men of Rome put forth their full strength; or to read in the Byzantine historians and in the controversial writings of the Fathers of the strange and half-forgotten life of the Eastern Empire. To cover much of this wide ground, one must read in a rather desultory way that will certainly be stigmatized as wanting in thoroughness and superficial: and yet the information acquired by this desultory reading may possibly be of more value than that of the orthodox student who has made a minute study of the most approved works of the most approved authors, but is dependent on manuals and magazine-articles for his knowledge of all the rest. And apart from the literary writings of the Greeks and Romans, there is much interesting reading in their inscriptions. When an inscription comes to light, it is very soon published in one of the journals or reviews devoted to such matters; and so becomes just as accessible as a literary work of the ancients which has been printed: questions of decipherment and restoration alone remaining in the one case, just as questions of the reading and collation of manuscripts alone remain in the other. The publication of an inscription is usually in this form:—first, there is a statement about the size and sort of the stone on which it is inscribed, the place of its discovery, and so forth; then follows the text of the inscription, printed line for line as it is cut on the stone, with gaps where the stone is broken away or defaced, the whole being set up in the form of inscription-type which comes nearest to the lettering of the original; next comes the text of the inscription, set up in ordinary type, the words separated and the sentences punctuated, with suggested restorations of the lost parts enclosed in brackets in the text; and finally there are notes on the purport of the inscription and its date, and on the persons and places and things mentioned. The inscriptions thus published are from time to time collected into great works, where they are duly classified and arranged.

For Latin inscriptions, there is the *Corpus Inscriptionum Latinarum* in fourteen volumes edited by Henzen, Mommsen and de Rossi: and with this goes a volume edited by Hübner in which the most remarkable inscriptions are given in facsimile instead of in inscription-type. For Greek inscriptions, there is the *Corpus Inscriptionum Græcarum* in four volumes edited by Böckh; and more recently the *Corpus Inscriptionum Atticarum*, also in four volumes, edited by Kirchhoff and Köhler, which incorporates the important discoveries of late years around Athens: and there is also the *Collection of ancient Greek Inscriptions in the British Museum*, edited by Sir Charles Newton. Anyone who wishes to know something of inscriptions will do well to go straight to one of these great works and turn over the pages and read, or try to read, as he goes the inscriptions which look short and easy and interesting, and then those which look a little less promising, and so on: and in this way he will very soon find out more about inscriptions than any books about them can teach him. Besides the inscriptions of the Greeks and Romans, their coins can now be very thoroughly studied in books, thanks to new processes for printing from photographs. It is best to begin with Mr Percy Gardner's *Types of Greek Coins* or with the illustrated edition of Mr Barclay Head's *Guide to the Coins of the Ancients:* and then to proceed to the latter writer's *Historia Numorum* (an English book) for a survey of the whole subject, and to his separate works on the coinages of Syracuse, Ephesos, etc., for minute studies of its details. There are the coinages of some thirteen hundred cities to be examined, some of them very varied and extending through long periods of history; and all sorts of questions are raised by the devices and inscriptions on the coins and by their weights: so it is quite possible to spend a good deal of time on the subject. The engraved gems of the Greeks and Romans might be studied in books almost as well as their coins, if the same processes had been employed for printing plates of them: but at present this has not been done except in isolated cases. A compact guide by Mr A. S. Murray with satisfactory plates is however nearly ready. Mr King's

Antique Gems and Rings should be consulted for fuller information, though its plates are poor: and it will be found a most entertaining book. Sculpture also might be very thoroughly studied in books: for a plate that gives two views of a statue from different points, and reproduces all the play of light and shade and all the varied tints upon the surface, is hardly inferior for most purposes to the statue itself; and such plates are produced, though their cost hinders their employment in ordinary works. Plaster casts, on the other hand, which are now very generally employed to illustrate sculpture, are of little service. A few years back the sole use of these casts (except as cheap ornaments for places of popular resort) was that when two pieces of sculpture, which were nearly related, or two portions of the same work had found their way to different collections, each could be supplemented by a cast of the other; and this was intelligible enough. Then came the formation of great museums of casts to illustrate the whole range of ancient sculpture: and these were useful for some limited purposes; measurements, for instance, for a comparison of various systems of proportion. But the small collections, which have been springing up everywhere of late, are useless for these purposes; and are meanwhile destroying any sense for beauty that may exist in this country. Ancient statues modelled with immense cleverness for effects of light and shade on the surface of the marble or the bronze are simply caricatured by these casts; distorted by shrinkage and hand-finishing, and wearying the eye with their uniform dull glare of white plaster. For the chief strength of Greek art lay in touches so slight that they are hardly noticed themselves and yet somehow transform the effect of a whole work; and anyone who does not realise this, will do well to learn from Mr Penrose's *Principles of Athenian Architecture* how infinitesimally small is the step from the most sublime buildings of the age of Pericles to the most ridiculous modern works in the Classical style. But happily there is plenty of ancient sculpture at hand to counteract the effect of the casts: partly scattered about in country houses and elsewhere (and for this the *Catalogue of Ancient Marbles in Great*

Britain by Michaelis is a fairly good guide) but chiefly
collected in the British Museum; and that great collection is
most worthy of study, for it consists mainly of Greek originals,
whereas the galleries in Italy are filled with copies made at
Rome in the earlier years of the Empire. For this whole
subject Mr A. S. Murray's *History of Greek Sculpture* should
be read. For painting, however, and for the minor arts,
there are not any satisfactory books: and one must examine
for oneself the examples in museums, and glean such information as one may from catalogues. Of course it is not
implied that any amount of reading about sculpture or gems
or coins or inscriptions could make a study of the things
themselves unnecessary: but as the books can be read when
and where one pleases, while the things must be studied at
stated times and places, it is generally convenient to get from
the books as much of one's information as one can. It is
however just as well, if one gives much time to these matters,
to have a few coins and antiquities of one's own: for one
learns more by having a few such things constantly at hand
than from an occasional survey of a number together in a
museum. And this is not an expensive affair: the museums
and the great collectors compete for works of exceptional
interest; but there is little demand for ordinary works, and
their prices are proportionately low. At the same time there
is always some risk of buying things that have been touched
up or are altogether modern: but then nothing ever makes
one an acute observer of the subtleties of ancient work so
thoroughly as a discovery that some coin or antiquity, for
which one has given a long price, is after all quite modern.
But beyond all the knowledge that may be gained from books
and from collections, it is very necessary to know something
of Greece and the Ægean and the shores of Asia Minor and
also of Sicily and Southern Italy, if one would understand
the ancient world or even its literature. Travelling is easy
now, and Rome may be reached in two days and Constanti-
nople or Athens in four days: and though it is pleasant to go
often and to stay long, one short visit to the Classic lands
is really sufficient; for any mind that can feel their influence

at all, will feel it at once. Those who cannot go, may find they can learn more from Bädeker and other guides than from all books of travels; for these, with very few exceptions, are simply incomplete autobiographies. Now all these things above named, this travelling, this knowledge of inscriptions and coins and antiquities, and this wide reading of Greek and Latin writers, are certainly most unpromising subjects for systematic instruction and for examination: and consequently they lie almost entirely beyond the present contracted scope of Classical learning in this country. But nevertheless they will repay study now: and if by some good fortune Classical education should be abandoned, they will still remain the study of all those who would know something of that ancient civilization under whose influence our modern world is so unconsciously living and must continue to live for many generations to come.

1—119. *Greek Painted Vases of Terra-Cotta.*

Greek painted vases deserve attention for two reasons: because they are themselves a striking product of Greek art; and because the paintings on them throw much light on the worships and legends and the daily life of the Greeks. They have generally been found in tombs, where they had been buried with their owners. When they were first brought to light again, they were mostly found in Etruria, and for many years they were considered Etruscan: but they have since been found in Greece itself and throughout the Greek world, and have been recognized as Greek. The earliest vases found in Greek soil have been found at Troy and Mycenæ and in the islands of the Ægean. Their age and origin is much disputed: most probably they are Carian work of about 700 B.C.; but they need not be discussed here, as they are not represented in the collection. From about 650 B.C. to 500 B.C. two styles flourished side by side: the first powerfully influenced by a knowledge of Oriental art obtained through the Greek settlers in the Delta of the Nile and in Cyprus: and the second slightly influenced by the Oriental tendency of the first. The vases of the first of these styles have rotund and slouching forms; and their decoration consists mainly of friezes of foreign or monstrous creatures, leopards and sphinxes and sirens, with Assyrian rosettes in the background: see nos. 1—14. The vases of the second of these styles have upright and angular forms; and their decoration is confined to a few rectangular spaces filled with patterns of straight lines or with stiff drawings of well known animals, goats and horses and geese, with little angular ornaments in the background: see no. 19. Some minor local styles flourished at the same time: notably that of Cyprus, in which globular vases are decorated with patterns of circles in black on a red or white surface: see no. 21. All these early styles were supplanted about 500 B.C. by a style first introduced at Athens some fifty years before. The making of vases was of importance there: two quarters of the city were named from the potteries, the Inner and the Outer Cerameïcos; and the sacred olive oil, which formed a prize at the Panathenaic Festival, was given to the victors in painted vases of terracotta. Some of these vases are still extant; and the oldest of them all can be of little later date than the institution of the Greater Panathenæa in 566 B.C. Its purpose is marked by the inscription ΙΜϽ:ΜΟꓕΟΑΜΟϽΜϽΘΑΜΟΤ painted upon it, reading, "Among the prizes from Athens am I." The same type continued in use for prize vases for more than two centuries, for some of them bear the names of Archons who were in office between 400 and 300 B.C. Vases of this type, but without inscriptions, seem to have been made for sale and export: see nos. 23, 24. This new style borrowed something of the upright and angular forms of vases, and of the rectangular spaces on them for decoration, from the second of the earlier styles mentioned above; and much of the method of painting from the first: but groups of human figures were substituted for rows of animals or monsters, and the backgrounds were cleared of ornaments: and at the same time the workmanship was vastly improved throughout: see nos. 23—45. About 500 B.C. another new style was introduced at Athens, in which the old system of painting was just reversed: instead of painting the figures black and leaving the background the colour of the clay, they painted the background black and left the figures the colour of the clay: see nos. 50—60. These two styles flourished side by side at Athens for half a century; but the black figure was at last generally abandoned for the red. It was at this period, in the interval between the Persian and the Peloponnesian Wars, that the great vase-painters lived. All that is known of them comes from inscriptions on vases, and chiefly on vases of the form termed *cylix*: see nos. 40, 52—54. There are three types of these inscriptions, and sometimes all three are found on a single vase: thus +A+PVLION ErOIEϟEN and EVΦPONIOϟ EΛPAΦϟEN and LEAΛPOϟ KALOϟ, shewing that the vase was made by Chachrylion and painted by Euphronios and dedicated to Leagros: and the various combinations of names on doubly and trebly inscribed vases shew that the great painters formed a very intimate society, beginning with Nicosthenes and Epictetos and ending with Euphronios, Duris, Hieron and Brygos a generation later. Many uninscribed vases of these painters can be recognized by their style alone: see nos. 52—56. The vases of this time, with their purity of outline and design and their extreme simplicity, are the finest ever made: see nos. 55, 56: the elaborate paintings on others, though masterly in themselves, being slightly misplaced: see nos. 50, 51. In some of the black-figured vases of about 500 B.C. the clay was covered with a white coating, and the figures were painted on this: see nos. 46—49: later on the figures were simply outlined on the white: and still later, about 400 B.C., they were painted in natural colours on the white: see nos. 61—64. Vases of this class are somewhat rare: the paintings on them are of funereal subjects, and their usual shape is one peculiarly associated with the grave. After 400 B.C. the art of vase painting began to decline. First, unmanageable subjects were attempted, which could not be treated satisfactorily except on large and flat surfaces; and the old skilfulness in adapting suitable subjects to the shapes of the vases was lost: and then the drawing and painting became careless, and finally clumsy: see nos. 65—86. Secondly, the shapes of metal vases were adopted, the clay was concealed under a coat of lustrous black paint, and reliefs instead of paintings were used for decoration : in fact, the vases became simply imitations of metal work : see nos. 88—115. Vase making was gradually abandoned at Athens, though it lingered on for many years in South Italy : and about 200 B.C. it died out altogether. There is great doubt about the names by which the various shapes of vases were known to the Greeks themselves : but practically it would be most inconvenient to alter, even for the better, the Greek names which are now in general use. The most curious shape, copied from the heads of men or beasts, is termed rhyton : see no. 82. In this catalogue, the name of the shape is given first in the description of each vase : the number at the end of each description gives the height in inches ; and if there are two numbers, the first gives the height and the second the breadth.

1—14. Greek vases of cream-coloured terra-cotta, with designs painted in black and at places in purple and white laid on over the black, details being marked by lines cut through the paint into the clay.

1. Hydria. Two friezes of animals : above, boar, leopard, leopard-headed bird, leopard, owl : below, boar, leopard, goat, goat, leopard, owl. 7¼.

2. Oinochoê. Frieze of animals : lion, leopard, swan, leopard, swan. 8¼.

3. Oinochoê. Frieze of animals : leopard, swan, goat, goat, lion, goat. 8⅝. *From the island of Rhodes.*

4. Oinochoê. Pattern of lines. 5¼. It has a lid fitting into its trefoil mouth.

5. Oinochoê. Pattern rubbed out. 4.

6. Oinochoê. Pattern rubbed out. 3⅞.

7. Oinochoê. Pattern of lines. 4.

8. Aryballos. The body reeded, and partly painted black. 6.

9. Bombylios. A cock with outspread wings. 7⅝. *From Camtros in the island of Rhodes.*

10. Bombylios. Two cocks: between them, an Assyrian ornament representing the Sacred Tree or Asheerah. 3¼. *Also from Camîros.*

11. Cotyliscos. Pattern of lines. 5¼. *From Veii in Etruria.*

12. Cotyliscos. Pattern rubbed out. 3⅝.

13. Cotyliscos. Pattern rubbed out. 3¾.

14. Lepastê. Frieze of five swans. 2½. 4⅜.

15—18. Greek vases of cream-coloured terra-cotta with patterns of lines and dots painted in black.

15. Phialê. The rim curved inward: one handle. 1¼. 3.

16. Pinax. ⅝. 5½.

17. Cone perforated through its axis. 1¼. Perhaps part of a vase, or a whorl.

18. Vase in form of a hare. 2. 3½.

19. Figure of a horse in cream-coloured terra-cotta partly painted black. 4¼. This must once have been one of the handles on the flat cover of an early Athenian vase of the form termed *lebes.*

20. Fragment of vase of cream-coloured terra-cotta. Plain.

21. Oinochoê of white terra-cotta with patterns of lines and circles in the Cyprus style. 3⅝.

22. Amphoriscos of white terra-cotta. The base pointed: no handles. 7¾.

23—45. Vases, chiefly Athenian, of orange-coloured terra-cotta with designs painted in lustrous black and at places in purple and white laid on over the black, details being marked by lines cut through the paint into the clay.

23—25. Amphorai. The body of the vase painted wholly black except for a panel in the front and another at the back and for a band of ornament round the neck and another round the base.

23. Panathenaic Amphora. In panel, Athene Promachos, robed, and armed with the Ægis, helmet, shield and

spear: on each side of her a Doric column and on it a cock. *Back.* In panel, three horsemen racing. 17⅞. *Much repainted.*

24. Panathenaic Amphora. Same as on 23. *Back.* In panel, three men racing on foot. 15⅛. It has its lid. *Much repainted.*

25. Ancient Etruscan copy of an Athenian amphora. In panel, two satyrs dancing: between them, a woman playing the double pipes: branches in background. *Back.* In panel, two satyrs dancing: between them, another playing the double pipes. The clay is pale yellow. The black paint has failed in the firing and come out red. No purple or white is used. The bands of ornament are omitted. 16½. It has its lid.

26—29. Amphorai. A group of figures in the front and another at the back, and large ornaments at the sides under the handles: bands of ornament running round the neck and round the lower part of the vase.

26. Dionysos, ivy-crowned and robed, holding a drinking-horn. Facing him, a dancing satyr. On each side of them, a dancing mænad, ivy-crowned and robed. Branches in background. *Back.* Dionysos, ivy-crowned and robed, holding a drinking-horn and riding on a mule. On each side of him, a satyr; and on the left, a mænad, robed. Branches in background. 15½. It has its lid. *From Vulci in Etruria.*

27. Combat of three warriors in full armour, the central combatant sinking on one knee. *Back.* Dionysos, ivy-crowned and robed, holding a drinking-horn and riding on a mule. On each side of him, a satyr. Branches in background. 17¼. It has its lid. *Also from Vulci.*

28. Three armed Amazons on horseback. Branches in background. *Back.* A man in full armour, and three others, robed, one of whom is seated on a folding-stool and holds a drinking-horn. Branches in background. 9¾.

29. Heracles strangling the Nemean lion. *Back.* The Chimæra. Trees and branches on both sides. 6¾. *Much repainted.*

30. Pelicê. Purple bands. No design. 11¾.

31—38. Lecythoi. A group of figures or design in

front: round the neck, a band of ornament: the lower part of the vase painted black.

31. Battle of the Gods and Giants: Athene slaying Ephialtes. On each side of them, a combatant. Branches in background. Athene is robed and armed with helmet, shield and spear. The rest are in full armour. 7¾. *From the island of Melos.*

32. An Amazon mounted on a white horse fighting a warrior in full armour on foot. On each side of them, a man, robed, and holding a staff. 7¼.

33. Subject effaced. 5½.

34. Dionysos, robed, holding a cup of the form termed *cantharos*. On each side of him, a satyr, one playing the double pipes, the other holding a drinking-horn. Branches in background. 6⅜.

35. Subjects effaced. 7¼.

36. Honeysuckle-pattern. 5½.

37. Honeysuckle-pattern. 4½.

38. Two large eyes: between them, a lion. 3½.

39. Lecythos. In front, a youth on horseback holding a spear: on each side of him, two men, robed, and holding spears. On neck, a floral ornament: on each side of it, a man, robed. 8½.

40. Cylix. Inside, Gorgon's head. *Outside,* in front and at back, two large eyes: between them, Dionysos, ivy-crowned and robed, holding drinking-horn. Branches in background. 3. 8¼.

41. Cylix. Lip recurved. No design. 3. 5¼.

42. Cyathis. Two large eyes: between them a dancing mænad, robed. Branches in background. Beyond the eyes, two lions regardant. 2⅞. 5.

43. Cyathis. Two armed men dancing the Pyrrhic dance. 3⅛. 4⅛.

44. Scyphos. Purple bands. No design. 4⅛. 5⅛.

45. Scyphos. In front and at back also: team of four horses in a chariot with an Amazon on each side, the whole between two sphinxes. 7⅛. 8⅞.

46—49. Greek vases of orange-coloured terra-cotta partly covered by a layer of pipe-clay on which the design is painted in black, details being marked by lines cut through the paint into the clay. The rest of the vase is either painted black, or has ornaments in black on its orange-coloured surface.

46. Lecythos. Wreath of laurel. 4⅛.
47. Lecythos. Wreath of ivy. 5½.
48. Lecythos. Wreath of ivy. 7⅛.
49. Scyphos. Three draped figures riding on hippocamps alternately with three draped figures dancing. Branches in background. Some of the black paint has turned red in the firing. No handles. 3⅜. 4⅛.

50—60. Vases, chiefly Athenian, of red terra-cotta. The body of the vase is painted a lustrous black except for groups of figures in the front and at the back (or in the front only) which are left in the colour of the clay. Details are marked upon the red by lines of black and sometimes of purple as well, and upon the black by purple. Sometimes the groups of figures are enclosed in panels by bands of ornament, and in this case the neck and base of the vase are generally surrounded by bands of ornament also : but more often there is merely a short line of ornament below the feet of the figures in each group.

50. Cratêr, with columnar handles. In panel Caineus and the Centaurs.—When Peirithoös king of the Lapiths wedded Hippodameia, the Centaurs were bidden to the marriage-feast. There they fought with the Lapiths and slew certain of them : but Caineus, a prince of the Lapiths, they could not slay, since he was invulnerable. And therefore they sought to bury him with rocks and trees. In the end, the Centaurs were worsted, mainly by the aid of Theseus.—Caineus, who is already buried nearly to his waist, stabs from below a Centaur who is about to hurl a mass of rock upon him. On each side of them, a Centaur holding up a tree with which to strike Caineus. Two of the Centaurs wear lion-skins round their necks: Caineus is in full armour.— This subject occurs on two extant pieces of Greek sculpture, the frieze of the Temple of Apollo Epicourios at Phigaleia

2

(begun soon after 430 B.C.) which is now in the British Museum, and the frieze of the Temple of Theseus at Athens (begun soon after 468 B.C.) which is still at Athens. But the powerful foreshortening of the Centaur to the left of the group suggests that its original was not a piece of sculpture but a painting, perhaps one of the frescoes by Micon in the Temple of Theseus. *Back.* In panel, a woman, robed, seized by two satyrs, one of whom carries a thyrsos. 19⅞.

51. Pelicê. In panel, Theseus slaying the Minotaur who is about to hurl a rock at him. *Back.* In panel, Theseus slaying Procrustes with an axe. 11¼. *See no. 52.*

52. Cylix. Inside: in centre, Theseus dragging the corpse of the Minotaur through a gateway: round it, 1. Theseus slaying Sciron with his foot-bath, 2. Theseus slaying Sinis with the branch of a tree, 3. Theseus slaying the sow of Crommyon which is defended by the nymph Phaia, 4. Theseus slaying Cercyon in a wrestling-match, 5. Theseus slaying Procrustes with an axe, 6. Theseus seizing the bull of Marathon. *Outside.* Nos. 5 and 3 repeated in the front, and nos. 2 and 1 at the back. These seven contests, together with the slaying of Periphetes, are the subjects of the eight sculptured metopes on the North and South sides of the Temple of Theseus at Athens. The club shewn between 4 and 5 in the inside, and between 5 and 3 on the outside, is probably the club of Periphetes: thus introduced to indicate the missing subject. 2⅝. 7. *From Nola.* Ten similar vases are known, one of which is signed by Duris and another by Euphronios. This must be the lost vase, formerly in a collection at Siena: in which case only nine others are known.

53. Cylix. Inside: a youth holding a cylix in one hand and with the other dipping a vase into a large cratêr which is wreathed with ivy. *Outside.* Both in the front and at the back, three youths, wearing cloaks and shoes, leaning on their staffs. A column and objects hanging up indicate a covered place. On the column, ΛΙϹ...ΚΑΛΟϹ, *Fair is Aisias* (?). Apparently by some painter of the school of Epictetos. 3¾. 9¼. *From Chiusi (Clusium) in Etruria.*

54. Cylix. Inside: an armed man, running, and treading on a shield. *Outside.* Both in the front and at the back, two youths boxing, one of whom is down, and another youth wearing a cloak and carrying a rod as umpire. The boxers wear the cæstus on their fists. The form of the vase is that generally employed by Brygos. 4. 9.

55. Amphora, with twisted handles. A satyr holding in one hand a helmet and in the other a pair of greaves, which are on a wooden stand with a leather handle. *Back.* A satyr with a spear in his right hand and a shield on his left arm. Much in the style of Duris. 18⅘.

56. Oinochoê. A youth holding a hoop in his left hand and the stick in his right. Much in the style of Hieron. 9¼.

57. Lecythos. A winged female figure, flying, with outstretched arms. 4.

58. Pelicê. Erôs, winged, with a casket in his hands, flying over an altar on which an offering is burning. *Back.* Youth, robed, holding a phialê. 4⅘.

59. Hydria. Three women, robed; those on either side standing and looking toward the central figure who is seated on a chair with a basket at her side and spinning with a distaff. 9.

60. Oinochoê. A youth reclining on a couch with pillows under his arm and a coverlet over his legs. On either side of him, a male figure approaching, wearing a chlamys and carrying an oinochoê: one is a youth; the other is bearded. White paint is used for the pillows and coverlet. 8⅞.

61—64. Athenian Lecythoi of red terra-cotta. The neck and base are painted a lustrous black, the rest of the vase is covered with a layer of pipeclay on which the design is painted in colours.

61. A monumental pillar adorned with black fillets, on one side of which is a youth, robed, and carrying two spears, and on the other side is a maiden fastening a diadem round her hair with both hands—much in the attitude of the statue of the Diadumenê. Such groups are sometimes ex-

2—2

plained as the meeting of Orestes and Electra at the tomb of Agamemnon. 15⅝.

62. A similar group, but the youth has no spears and the maiden turns toward the pillar. 11¾.

63. A similar group, but the youth holds a casket or basket in his hands. 13¼.

64. A similar group, but the youth, who is not robed, kneels looking toward the pillar which is adorned with scarlet fillets. 9.

65—82. Vases, chiefly South Italian, of red terra-cotta. The body of the vase is painted a lustrous black except for groups of figures and large floral ornaments. White and yellow paint are used in places.

65. Cratêr, with columnar handles. In panel, a man and a youth, each reclining on a couch and spinning a cylix in the game of cottabos: at the foot of the man's couch sits another youth, playing the lyre: all half-draped. Footstools below the couches. *Back.* In panel, a youth playing the double pipes, between two others leaning on staffs: all robed. Round the neck (in black upon a red ground) four goats and four leopards alternately. 14¾.

66. Cratêr. A woman seated between two youths, one holding a thyrsos, and the other carrying a spear: all half-draped. *Back.* Dionysos, half-draped, seated and holding a thyrsos: on each side of him, a woman, robed, one of whom holds a casket and a thyrsos. Two large birds over the handles, and another in front. 12⅝. *Much restored.*

67. Pelicê. A youth reclining on a couch, on which is seated a woman, half-draped. On either side of them, a woman, robed, and a satyr: above them, Erôs, flying: below, a quail. *Back.* A woman, robed, and a youth, who carries a thyrsos. On either side of them, a satyr. Below them, a quail. 20.

68. Cratêr, with handles terminating below in swan's heads and adorned above with masks in relief. Below a portico, a woman, robed and seated: before her, a youth who fans her. On each side of the portico, a woman, robed, bringing mirror, necklace, etc. Above (on the neck of the

vase) a woman, robed, seated and holding a fan. *Back.* A monumental pillar adorned with fillets: on each side of it a woman, robed, bringing offerings. 24⅜.

69. Cratêr. A woman, half draped, dancing between two others, robed. *Back.* Two women, robed: one of them seated. 14⅝.

70. Cratêr. A youth, wearing a chlamys and holding a phialê, facing a young satyr who holds a basket. *Back.* Two youths, robed; one leaning on his staff. 9⅜.

71. Hydria. A woman, robed and seated, holding a mirror before her face. Facing her, a youth, half draped, holding a phialê and a wreath. 12¼.

72. Lecythos. A youth, holding a phialê, facing a maiden, robed and holding a casket. Between them a pillar, perhaps funereal. 12¾.

73. Oinochoê. In panel, a woman, half-draped, seated and holding a phialê. Facing her, a woman, robed, holding a mirror and a wreath. 9¼.

74. Oinochoê. A female head. 7⅝.

75. Olpê. A female head, between outspread wings. 4.

76. Phialê Mesomphalos of orange-coloured terra-cotta. Inside, painted black in centre and at rim: between these, radiating lines of black and orange and a circle of white dots. 1½. 8½.

77. Aryballos. A female head. 2¾.

78. Cylix. Inside: a female head, surrounded by a laurel-wreath. *Outside.* A laurel-wreath. 1¾. 6.

79. Pyxis, with its cover. On each, two female heads. 4½. 3¾.

80. Pyxis. Two female heads. 2. 4¼.

81. Cylix. Inside: ivy-wreath. *Outside.* Both in the front and at the back, two youths, half-draped, one carrying a shield and the other a spear. 2½. 4⅞.

82. Rhyton, in the form of a griffin's head. Upon the neck, a winged hermaphrodite, seated and holding a phialê. 7½.

83—86. Vases, chiefly South Italian, of red terra-cotta. The body of the vase is painted a lustrous black, and upon this designs are painted in white, yellow and maroon, and also marked by incised lines.

83. Scyphos. Floral and other ornaments. $3\frac{3}{4}$. $3\frac{1}{8}$.

84. Cylix. Floral and other ornaments. $2\frac{3}{8}$. $4\frac{1}{8}$.

85. Pelicê. Floral ornaments, and on one side a female head. 4.

86. Olpê. Mæander-pattern round the neck. $4\frac{3}{4}$.

87. Cantharos of red terra-cotta. The body of the vase is painted a lustrous black except for portions of a panel in the front and another at the back, in which floral and other ornaments are painted in white on the red and black and in black on the red. $4\frac{1}{2}$.

88—115. Greek vases of red terra-cotta painted entirely with a lustrous black and sometimes bearing ornaments in low relief or stamped in.

88. Amphoriscos, with reeded sides. $5\frac{7}{8}$.

89. Oinochoê, with reeded sides. $4\frac{3}{8}$.

90. Epichysis. On the handle is moulded in relief a human figure from the waist upward bending backward: and at the foot of the handle, a mask. $6\frac{3}{4}$. A lump of iron has been soldered on to the handle in some conflagration.

91. Epichysis. $5\frac{1}{4}$. *From Cervetri (Cære) in Etruria.*

92. Aryballos, with reeded sides. 5.

93. Aryballos. 3.

94. Olpê. 6.

95. Olpê. $2\frac{7}{8}$.

96. Olpê. $2\frac{3}{8}$.

97. Olpê. 2.

98. Vase with reeded sides, perforated top, handle and spout. $3\frac{7}{8}$.

99. Askos. At top, bearded head in relief. 2. $3\frac{1}{2}$.

100. Askos. At top, head of Heracles wearing lion skin in relief. $1\frac{5}{8}$. $3\frac{1}{4}$.

101. Cantharos. Inside, honeysuckle-pattern impressed. $2\frac{7}{8}$.

102. Pinax. Inside, a small Gorgon's head surrounded by elaborate honeysuckle and other ornaments impressed. $2\frac{1}{2}$. $9\frac{3}{8}$.

103. Pinax. $3\frac{1}{2}$. $7\frac{1}{2}$.

104. Pinax. $3\frac{3}{8}$. 8.

105. Pinax. 2. $3\frac{3}{8}$. *From Viterbo (Surrina) in Etruria.*

106. Pinax. $1\frac{7}{8}$. $6\frac{1}{2}$.

107. Scyphos. $3\frac{1}{2}$. $4\frac{1}{4}$.

108. Cylix. $3\frac{1}{8}$. $5\frac{3}{4}$.

109. Cylix, with twisted handles. $3\frac{1}{2}$. $4\frac{5}{8}$.

110. Cylix. $1\frac{3}{4}$. $5\frac{1}{8}$. Letters incised underneath.

111. Cylix. 2. $5\frac{7}{8}$.

112. Cylix. Inside, honeysuckle-pattern impressed. $1\frac{7}{8}$. $5\frac{5}{8}$. *From Chiusi.*

113. Cylix, with a cover. $2\frac{1}{2}$. $4\frac{1}{2}$. *From Athens.*

114. Cylix, with one handle. 2. $3\frac{1}{4}$.

115. Cylix, without handles. Inside, in high relief, a youthful head with long hair bound in a diadem, seen nearly in full face. Round it, a band of ornament impressed. $1\frac{3}{4}$. $5\frac{1}{4}$.

116—119. Fragments of vases painted with lustrous black.

116. From Girgenti (Agrigentum).

117. From Carthage.

118. From Carthage.

119. From Tiryns.

120—167. *Etruscan Moulded Vases of Terra-Cotta.*

The Etruscans imported painted vases from Greece to a large extent; and they attempted, to a very small extent and with very limited success, to produce painted vases in the Greek style: see no. 25 above. But for moulded vases, they had a style of their own: and they employed these moulded vases, jointly with the painted vases from Greece, in furnishing their tombs. These moulded clay vases, which have been found at Chiusi (the ancient *Clusium*) in large numbers, are simply imitations of metal vases in shape and in decoration; and most probably they were never intended for use, but only for interment in tombs as substitutes for the real metal vases belonging to the deceased: see nos. 137—164. The Etruscans were famed for their metal work: and these vases are of some interest in illustrating that, though they are of little interest in other ways. They date from about 650 to 450 B.C. The very primitive vases, chiefly found at Veii, must be of earlier date. Most of them are in a rude style which was in use in many countries besides Etruria: see nos. 120—131: while others shew the transition from this to the metallic style: see nos. 132—136.

120—136. Etruscan black-ware from Veii.

120. Tripod. 2⅝. Plain.

121—131. Vases with incised decoration of lines, either continuous or dotted.

121. Olpê. 2¾. Dotted lines along handle.

122. Amphoriscos. 4¾. }
123. Amphoriscos. 4. } Pattern of zigzags and spirals.

124. Amphoriscos, without handles. 4⅜. Rows of vertical lines.

125. Oinochoê. 4. Rows of vertical lines: wedge-shaped ornaments above.

126. Stamnos. 2⅜. Lines round vase, and wedge-shaped ornaments.

127. Cylix. 2. 4¾. }
128. Cylix. 2⅛. 4½. } Lines round vase.

129. Cylix. 2. 4¾. }
130. Cylix. 2⅜. 4¼. } Lines round vase, and wedge-
131. Cylix. 2¼. 4½. } shaped ornaments.

132—136. Vases with impressed decoration of lines or circles.

132. Holmos. 3¼. 5¼. Lines round vase outside.

133. Cyathos. 1¼. 3⅜. Radiating lines, inside.

134. Vase shaped like an egg-cup. 2¼. Two rows of circles round rim.

135. Holmos. 5. 8⅞. Radiating lines, inside. Outside, round vase, lines and rows of circles: also dotted lines. On one side, a handle, moulded in the round, originally representing a man between two horses.

136. Cylix. 2¾. 6. Lines radiating from concentric circles, inside. Outside, lines round vase and wedge-shaped

ornaments, incised. The lower side is reeded, each reed ending in a knob. On each side, three flat knobs for handles.

137—164. Etruscan black-ware from Chiusi.

137. Cyathos. 4. 4. The lower side is reeded, each reed ending in a knob.

138. Holmos. 4. 6. The sides ribbed, as in basket-work.

139. Fragment of a vase covered with small knobs.

140. Holmos. 5. 6. A palm pattern of Assyrian character incised round vase.

141. Fragment of a similar vase.

142. Pinax. $1\frac{7}{8}$. 5. Round the rim, a modern inscription, incised in imitation of Etruscan.

143. Pinax. $1\frac{1}{8}$. 5. Plain.

144. Pinax. $1\frac{1}{8}$. 5. Plain.

145. Pinax. $1\frac{1}{8}$. $4\frac{1}{4}$. Plain.

146. Oinochoê. 7. Round it, incised lines. This was found at Veii, but it is of Chiusi ware.

147—154. Vases with rough reliefs from moulds applied by hand.

147. Patera, with tall twisted handles, to each of which are affixed four masks in relief, and standing on a tall columnar foot, which is not joined to the vase itself. 15. $11\frac{1}{4}$. Incised pattern of lines.

148. Amphora, with lid. $24\frac{1}{2}$. Two masks in relief upon the neck, and two others above the handles. Round the lower part of the vase, five sphinxes in relief. Inside the lid, impressed honeysuckle ornament.

149. Amphora, with lid. 13. Four masks in relief round the rim, and three winged horses round the lower part of the vase. Incised wedge-shaped ornaments round the neck, and impressed rope-pattern round the lid.

150. Lower part of a similar vase. $3\frac{5}{8}$. 4. Round it, six swans in relief: also incised zigzags.

151. Holmos. 8. $5\frac{7}{8}$. Round it, four swans alternately with four lotos-flowers, in relief: also incised zigzags.

152. Holmos, with lid, on which are four masks in relief. $5\frac{1}{2}$. 4.

153. Holmos. 3. $3\frac{1}{4}$. Round it, impressed rope-pattern.

154. Cantharos, with lid. $6\frac{1}{4}$. 6. Round it, six faces seen in profile, and on each handle two snake's heads, all in relief. On the lid, three winged male figures, seen from the waist upward, in relief: also, incised flower-patterns.

155—158. Holmoi, with friezes impressed by revolving cylindrical moulds, so that the design recurs at regular intervals.

155. Double lotos pattern. $3\frac{1}{2}$. $5\frac{3}{4}$.

156. Stag, lion, sphinx, pomegranate-tree, sphinx, lion, repeated. $4\frac{1}{4}$. 6.

157. Stag, sphinx, lion, winged man, lion, repeated. A fragment.

158. Man seated and holding a necklace in each hand, man standing, man seated and holding spear, four men standing, repeated. $5\frac{3}{4}$. $5\frac{5}{8}$.

159. Cyathis. $1\frac{1}{4}$. $2\frac{3}{8}$. In relief on the handle, a Siren holding two men in her arms.

160. Cyathis. $2\frac{5}{8}$. $3\frac{1}{4}$. In relief on the handle, a mask and above it a snake. Round the body, incised zigzags.

161. Spoon. 6. The handle in the form of a horse's leg.

162. Alabastron. $8\frac{5}{8}$. $1\frac{7}{8}$. Plain.

163. Pinax. $\frac{5}{8}$. $3\frac{3}{4}$. Plain.

164. Oinochoê. $1\frac{1}{4}$. Plain.

165—167. Etruscan vases of other wares.

165. Rim of a large flat dish of red-ware, round which are two friezes both stamped from the same revolving cylindrical mould. Leopard, stag, leopard, man with spear attacking a boar, tree, repeated. Diameter, 18.

166. Stamnos of red-ware. $2\frac{3}{4}$. *From Chiusi.* Apparently Sardinian.

167. Shallow vase, with eight knobs projecting from the sides. It is of cream-coloured terra-cotta, with concentric circles and groups of lines painted in red outside: and painted wholly red inside. The rim is pierced with two holes for hanging up. 2⅛. 6⅛. *From Veii.* Also, apparently Sardinian.

168—307. *Samian and Roman Red-Ware.*

Samos was celebrated among the Romans for the red-ware manufactured there: and hence they came to call their own red-ware Samian. This was in general use from about 100 B.C. to 400 A.D. throughout the countries then governed by the Romans. There are two sorts of it. First, plain vases without any decoration at all: these are generally stamped inside with the maker's name: see nos. 168—230. Secondly, embossed vases with figures of men and beasts or ornaments in low relief: these are seldom stamped with the maker's name: see nos. 231—302. The same groups and ornaments are commonly repeated several times on the same vase: the object being to cover the whole surface with decoration of some sort, rather than to employ decoration adapted to the form of the surface. This embossed red-ware must have been suggested by similarly embossed terra-cotta vases painted a lustrous black in imitation of metal. In the same way the strictly metallic decoration of the Etruscan black-ware was applied to a red-ware made by the Etruscans: see no. 165 above. There was an important manufactory of Roman red-ware at Arezzo (the ancient *Aretium*) and its products may sometimes be distinguished from the ordinary Samian: see nos. 303, 304.

168—178. Vases of plain Samian red-ware.

168. Dish. 2⅛. 10¼. REGENVS. *Regenus.*
169. Dish. 1½. 7½. COI...IVSF. *Conatius fecit.*
170. Dish. 1⅛. 6⅝. ⊛SEVERI. *Officina Severi.* See 213, 214.
171. Bowl. 2½. 5¼. MOMO. *Momi officina.* See 196.
172. Bowl. 2½. 4⅝. PASSI. *Passieni.* See 197.
173. Bowl. 2⅝. 5¼. Stamp illegible.
174. Bowl. 1⅜. 3⅞. Unstamped.

175. Bowl. 1⅜. 3⅜. Unstamped.
176. Bowl. 1¼. 3¾. Unstamped.
177. Bowl. 2. 6⅜. Unstamped. On one side the rim is shaped for pouring out.
178. Bowl. 1⅞. 5. Unstamped. In low relief round the rim, four buds with stalks and ten other stalks between them.

179—218. Fragments of vases of plain Samian red-ware with stamps.

179. .LBIM. *Albini manu.*
180. BORILLIM. *Borilli manu.*
181. CALAVAF. *Calava fecit.*
182. OF·CALVI. *Officina Calvi.*
183. CAPITOF. *Capitolinus fecit.*
184. CENTOR. *Centorinus.*
185. OFCOELI. *Officina Coelii.*
186. COSRVF. *Cosinius Rufinus fecit.*
187. OFCOTTO. *Officina Cotto...(?).*
188. CRESTI. *Cresti.*
189. DIVICATVS. *Divicatus.*
190. FELICIONIS. *Felicionis.*
191. FVSCI. *Fusci.*
192. OF·IVCVN. *Officina Jucundi.*
193. ..CINVSFC. *Licinus fecit.*
194. MARTIIO. *Martii officina.*
195. OF·MR·ER·F. *Officina Maternini, Errimus fecit*(?).
196. OMOM. *Officina Momi.* See 171.
197. PASSI. *Passieni.* See 172.
198. ...CLOSFE. *Paterclos fecit.*
199. PATRICI. *Patricii.* See 215.
200. PAVLIM. *Pauli manu.*
201. PO.IO. *Polio.*
202. .OL. *Polio.*
203. .FPOLIO. *Officina Polionis.*
204. OFPRIMI. *Officina Primi.*
205. OFPRIM. *Officina Primi.*
206. ..IM.·PATER. *Primulus Pater.*
207. FVGNIM. *Pugni manu.*

208. PUGM. *Pugni manu.*

209. Q. VAC. *Quinti Valerii C[aii filii Veriani?].*

210. SABINVS. *Sabinus.*

211. SACER·VASLF. *Sacer Vasili fecit.*

212. SATVRNNIO. *Saturnini officina.*

213. ⊕SEVERI. *Officina Severi.* See 170.

214. ⊕SEVERI. *Officina Severi.* See 170.

215. SILVIPARICI. *Silvii Patricii.* See 199.

216. VIDVCOS·F. *Viducos fecit.*

217. . IRTVTIS. *Virtutis.*

218. VTALISMSF. *Vitalis manu suâ fecit.*

219—227. Fragments with illegible stamps.

228—230. Fragments without stamps. In 228, the inner surface roughened with coarse sand during the making.

231. Bowl of embossed Samian red-ware: round it a band of ornament. 3. 6¼.

232—302. Small fragments of 69 vases of embossed Samian red-ware.

Nos. 168 and 171—178 are from Xanten (the ancient *Castra Vetera*) on the Rhine. Nos. 169, 170 and 179—298 are from various parts of London, except no. 194, which is from Somersetshire. Nos. 299—302 are from Rome.

303, 304. Aretine red-ware.

303. Patera. 1½. 5. Plain. Stamp: a foot wearing a sandal.

304. Patera. 1¼. 4¼. Plain. Unstamped.

305—307. Roman red-ware.

305. Patera, with raised foot and two small flat handles. 3¼. 9⅝.

306. Patera, with tripod feet. 3⅝. 6⅞.

307. Olpê. 6⅛.

308—449. *Bronzes.*

Bronze was much used by the Greeks in sculpture, and probably more of the great statues and bas-reliefs were made from bronze than from marble: but in later times there was a far larger demand for old metal than for lime, and ancient

sculpture of any considerable size is now far rarer in bronze
than in marble.   Greek statues in bronze are mostly hollow.
Generally, statuettes were cast in one piece: for statues, the
trunk and head and arms were cast separately, and then
fastened together: and huge figures, like the Colossos of
Rhodes which was 105 feet in height, were cast in many
pieces and built up gradually: see nos. 308—314 for statuettes.
But in early times (about 600 B.C.) statues were built up of
bronze plates bent into shape and nailed on to a wooden
trunk inside: and in those days the interior walls of important
buildings were sheathed with similar bronze plates, often
worked in relief: and the same sheathing was employed for
wooden objects: see nos. 445—449.   Bronze plates of various
shapes, worked in relief, were at all times employed as ornaments upon objects of all sorts: see no. 315 particularly.
The art of engraving on bronze with a burin flourished in
Etruria: and the Etruscan mirrors thus decorated form an
interesting study.   Many hundreds of these exist, mostly
dating from 450 to 300 B.C. see nos. 374—376.   Nearly all the
metal work found in Etruria and throughout the Greek world,
is bronze; arms and armour and axes as well as vases and
lamps and bracelets: and in those lands art and industry
were so closely allied that the very commonest of these
bronze objects are faultless in form, and are often adorned
with reliefs of merit.   The ancient colour of the bronzes is lost
beyond recovery; their present greenish hue arising from
decay.

308—315.   Bronze statuettes, etc.

308.   Statuette of Zeus. 6¾.   Round his head a laurel
wreath, fastened by a ribbon, the ends of which fall in
front of his shoulders.   Open sandals on his feet.   In his
right hand, a thunderbolt, broken.   The left arm, which is
broken off, must have been raised and resting on a tall
sceptre. *From Baalbek.*

309.   Statuette. 4½.   A male figure; the right arm
upraised and holding a weapon, which is broken off; a shield
on the left arm.

310. Statuette. $3\frac{1}{8}$. A male figure, robed, and holding a phialê in the right hand.

311. Statuette. $3\frac{1}{4}$. A male figure holding a phialê in the right hand.

312. Bust of Athenê. 3. She wears a helmet with triple crest, and over her shoulders the Ægis with the Gorgoneion in front.

313. Bust of Zeus Sarapis. $2\frac{1}{2}$. Upon his head the modius. The bust ends below in an eagle with outspread wings.

314. Hand. $\frac{3}{4}$. From a statuette.

315. Relief. 3. $2\frac{3}{4}$. Victory with outspread wings, draped from the waist downward, placing a wreath on the head of a man, dressed as a Roman soldier and holding two spears in his right hand while he rests his left hand on his shield. Probably from the scabbard of a sword.

316—339. Bronze vases, etc.

316. Phialê Mesomphalos. $2\frac{3}{4}$. $12\frac{5}{8}$.

317. Another. $\frac{7}{8}$. $5\frac{1}{4}$.

318. Phialê. $2\frac{1}{8}$. $8\frac{1}{8}$.

319. Phialê. 2. $10\frac{1}{2}$. It has a massive handle at one side, and below it a leaf in relief.

320. Similar handle, but from a larger vase: below it a Gorgon's head in relief.

321. Phialê. 3. $7\frac{5}{8}$. It has at one side a long horizontal handle ending in a Satyr's mask in relief, the beard ending below in a foot to support the handle.

322. Strainer. $1\frac{3}{4}$. $5\frac{3}{4}$. It has a long horizontal handle bearing in relief floral ornaments and the figure of a winged man, seated, and holding some objects within his outstretched arms.

323. Strainer. 2. $5\frac{1}{2}$. The long horizontal handle ending in a ram's head.

324. Strainer. $1\frac{5}{8}$. $4\frac{7}{8}$. The handle plain. *From Chiusi.*

325. Strainer. $1\frac{1}{4}$. $4\frac{7}{8}$. The handle broken off.

326. Handle of a similar vase, ending in a head of Medusa in relief. $5\frac{3}{4}$. *From Catania.*

327. Oinochoê. 7½. The handle (which does not belong to the vase) ends above in a mask.

328. Similar handle, ending above in a female head and below in a head of Heracles wearing the lion's scalp. 6⅛.

329. Similar handle, ending above in a mask and outstretched arms and below in a mask and floral ornament between two smaller masks. 5½. *From Veii.*

330. Similar handle, ending below in a floral ornament. 8⅝.

331. Same as 330. 7½.

332. Olpê. 4¾.

333. Olpê. 4⅜.

334. Bucket. 5. It has a moveable handle. *From Cervetri.*

335. Double moveable handles of a similar vase, with the plates into which they fitted.

336. A similar handle. *From Chiusi.*

337. Another, with twisted pattern.

338. Another, with twisted pattern.

339. Another, from a very small vase.

340—348. Ornaments to be attached to vases, boxes, etc.

340. Mask, with ring above. 3.

341. Mask. 1¼.

342. Mask. 1¼.

343. Mask. 1½.

344. Ram's head. 1¾.

345. Square ornament. 1¼.

346. Triangular ornament. 2⅛. Probably, trappings from a horse's harness.

347. Leaf-ornaments. 2½.

348. Leaf-ornaments. 1½.

349—357. Series of celts, or axes, shewing the progress of the art of making them.

349—351. Broad and short, the surface plain, without means of fastening to the handle.

352. Narrower and longer, the sides turned slightly up to fasten to the handle.

353. The blade widening out almost to a semicircle.

354. A bar across the centre to prevent the blade being forced back into the handle by a blow.

355. The sides more turned up.

356, 357. Hollow, with an opening at the back into which the handle fits. On one side a ring for further fastening by a thong.

358—360. Spear-heads.

358. 4$\frac{1}{2}$. } Of bronze.
359. 4$\frac{3}{4}$. }
360. 5$\frac{1}{4}$. Of iron.

361. Arrow-head, apparently Carthaginian. *From Girgenti.*

362—365. Leaden sling bolts. No. 362 bears in relief on one side, a thunderbolt, on the other, RVF..IMP.; and is probably false: the rest are plain. *Nos. 362—364 from Perugia. No. 365 from the upper citadel of Samê in Cephalonia.*

366. Spiked ring for fitting on a staff.

367. Another, of iron.

368. Half a horse's bit.

369. Cattle-bell. 2$\frac{1}{2}$.

370. Flesh-hook with seven large prongs round a ring and an eighth prong and a smaller ring above. 12.

371. Iron sacrificial knife. 11$\frac{1}{4}$.

372. Strigil, with recurved handle. 9.

373. Strigil, with remains of an iron handle. 9.

374. Mirror. 9. Engraved on it, a young man, wearing a Phrygian cap, between two other young men: in the background a woman. Perhaps, Paris, Helen, and the Dioscuri.

375. Mirror. 9. Design effaced.

376. Handle of a mirror in the form of a youth. He has long hair: his right hand is raised to his head, his left is by his side and holds drapery falling from his shoulders. Round his neck is a bulla. 7.

377. Stylus. 7$\frac{5}{8}$.

378. A two-pronged fork. 5$\frac{3}{4}$.

3

379—400. Bracelets and rings.

379—386. Simply circular,

379.	$2\frac{1}{4}$.	With a series of knobs.	383.	$1\frac{1}{8}$.	Twisted.
380.	$2\frac{1}{4}$.		384.	$1\frac{1}{2}$.	Plain.
381.	$1\frac{7}{8}$.		385.	$1\frac{5}{8}$.	
382.	$1\frac{5}{8}$.		386.	$\frac{3}{4}$.	

387—390. The ends not quite meeting.

387. $3\frac{3}{8}$. Twisted.

388. $2\frac{3}{4}$, and 389. 2. Plain.

390. $3\frac{1}{2}$. Plain: the ends hooked, and joined by three links.

391—393. The ends overlapping: plain.

391. $2\frac{3}{8}$. 392. $2\frac{1}{8}$. 393. $1\frac{1}{4}$.

394—396. In spirals.

394. $1\frac{1}{2}$, and 395. $1\frac{1}{2}$. Two turns.

396. $2\frac{3}{8}$. Three turns, knobs at each end.

397—400. The spiral turned back so as to make four coils on one side and two on the other. Plain, but one end twisted.

397. $2\frac{5}{8}$. 399. $1\frac{3}{4}$.

398. $2\frac{1}{4}$. 400. $1\frac{1}{2}$.

401—410. Other personal ornaments.

401. Fibula. 3.

402—404. Parts of others.

405. Twisted pin. $17\frac{1}{4}$. *From Veii.*

406. Iron pin. $6\frac{1}{8}$.

407, 408. Buckles.

409, 410. Thimbles. *From Arles.*

411—434. Various small objects of bronze.

411. Bust of a head, suspended by a ring. $2\frac{1}{2}$. Probably from a steelyard.

412. Perforated plummet or weight. 1.

413—416. Very small plummets or weights.

417—419. Very small heads of foxes, the necks ending in hooks.

420. Bird flying, ring on back for suspension. $1\frac{2}{3}$.

421. Dolphin. $1\frac{2}{3}$.

422. Sheep. $\frac{3}{4}$.

423. Ox. $2\frac{1}{2}$.

424. Ram. $2\frac{3}{4}$. The legs fasten into a flat piece of bronze.

425. Figure of a horse. 5. Part of a horse's bit.

426. Curved neck of a bird, ending in a loop. Also, part of a horse's bit.

427. Very small loop with a ring attached.

428. Floral ornament. 3.

429. Twisted pin with hook. $1\frac{3}{4}$.

430—432. Keys.

433, 434. Lock bolts.

435—444. Lamps, chains, etc.

435. Candelabrum. $37\frac{1}{4}$. Stem plain, with three feet, each ending in a claw: at top, four short branches, each ending in a spike from which to hang a lamp.

436. Lamp. 2. 6.

437. Lamp with two wick-holes, between which is a lion's head in relief. $1\frac{1}{2}$. 5. Three chains attach it to a ring, attached by another chain to another ring.

438. Lamp bowl. 5. 9. Attached by three chains of double links to a triangular plate above which is a ring. Round the bowl are three handles, from which hang rings, alternately with three masks above which the chains are fastened. *From Perugia.*

439. Lower end of a similar bowl.

440. Lamp bowl. 2. 3. Attached to a boss by three chains of links alternately small and large. *From Cortona.*

441. Ring. $\frac{1}{4}$. 5. Round it, eight small rings attached by bars to four similar rings which are attached by longer bars to another small ring: this last being attached by a hook to a small handle. The bars are hooked at both ends and covered by spirals of bronze wire. Parts are missing.

442. Very small chain with ball at end. 4.

443. Chain of 91 links, about a yard long. Each link is of two rings, but every other link has two extra rings hanging loose.

444. Chain of 53 links, about four yards long. The

3—2

links are heart-shaped : those in the centre are larger than those toward the ends.

445—449. Bronze sheathing of wooden objects. *From Veii.*

445. Ribbed. From a box. 3½. 7.
446. Panelled. From a box. 4. 3½.
447—449. From handles.

450—673. *Glass.*

Phœnician vases of variegated glass are often found in Greek tombs of earlier date than 450 B.C. : and it is clear that the Greeks prized these highly, for they used to mount them on gold stands : see nos. 469, 470. They are often thoroughly Greek in shape : and although most of them were no doubt made in the great glass-working city of Sidon, many were probably made at places like Ialysos in Rhodes where a few Phœnician settlers remained on after the appropriation of the district by Greek colonists. These vases are generally of a deep translucent blue glass; in the surface of which (while heated) a pattern has been grooved with a point, the grooves being subsequently filled in with strings of heated yellow or green glass, and the whole welded together by a further heating and then polished smooth on cooling down. The patterns always consist of lines; either spirals and zigzags running round the vase, or palm-leaves running up the sides. The later Greeks and the Romans made their variegated glass in another way : see nos. 471—563. A number of rods of different coloured glass were placed side by side, and welded together by heating : the united mass was then sliced up crosswise, each slice shewing the same coloured pattern; and by drawing out the mass lengthwise before slicing, the pattern could be reduced to any degree of minuteness. If a vase or bowl was to be made, a slice was heated and then blown to the required shape : and if a flat surface was to be ornamented, a slice was attached just as it was. The patterns are often geometrically regular : but there is often studied irregularity, to imitate the veining of marble or porphyry or serpentine and the like. For these effects, glass vases of a single colour were sometimes lightly splashed, while being blown into shape, with molten glass of other colours. The Romans made larger and coarser vases of ordinary clear glass or of plain blue, yellow, purple or green glass: but curiously these are now often more brilliantly coloured than the variegated vases: see nos. 450—468. This is simply the effect of decay: the surface peeling off in films fine enough to be affected by the differences of the wave-lengths corresponding to the several colours in the spectrum. Variegated glass was also much used for beads for stringing on necklaces: see nos. 564—637. To make such beads, slices from a welded mass of rods of various coloured glass were bevelled down to spherical or ovoid forms, so as to shew something of the colouring of the interior along the sides as well as at the ends. Plain coloured glass was used for such beads as well: and also for ornaments moulded on one side only and pierced for stitching on to dresses. Among other ancient uses of glass was the manufacture of ornaments with designs impressed in imitation of engraved gems: see nos. 666—673.

450—468. Vases of glass originally plain but now iridescent from decay.

450. Urn, with lid. 11$\frac{3}{8}$. *From Cumæ.*
451. Urn. 6$\frac{5}{8}$.
452. Square bottle with handle. 8.
453. Jug with handle. 6.
454. Bottle. 5$\frac{1}{4}$.
455. Bottle. 3$\frac{1}{4}$. Round it, a raised spiral. *From Chiusi.*
456. Bottle. 3$\frac{3}{4}$.
457. Bottle. 3$\frac{1}{8}$.
458. Bottle. 2.
459. Bottle. 2.
460. Narrow bottle. 4$\frac{1}{4}$.
461. Narrow bottle. 4$\frac{5}{8}$.
462. Cylindrical bottle. 3.
463. Bowl. 1$\frac{3}{4}$. 4.
464. Bowl. 1$\frac{1}{4}$. 4.
465. Bowl. 1$\frac{1}{4}$. 4.

466. Bottle. 5⅜. Of blue glass.   ⎫
467. Bottle. 2¼. Of blue glass.   ⎬   *From Chiusi.*
468. Bottle. 5¾. Of yellow glass. ⎭

469—563. Vases, etc., of variegated glass.

469. Oinochoê. 5⅛.
470. Amphoriscos. 2⅝.
471. Handle of a vase.
472. Neck of bottle.
473—475. Portions of large bowls with ribbed sides.
476—563. Fragments of bowls, etc.

564—637. Beads, and other objects pierced for stringing.

638—659. Buttons of coloured glass. Such buttons were formerly believed to be draughtsmen: but probably they are ornaments intended to be gummed on to wood-work.

660. Tail of a fish: clear glass, with incised lines.

661. Tail of a fish: white glass with overlaid spiral of blue glass.

662. Part of spoon handle: blue glass inlaid with white in a spiral.

663. Small glass plate with two loops, moulded on one side as a bunch of grapes.

664. Small ball of white glass decorated with knobs of red glass and fastened to an iron loop. *From Chiusi.*

665. Pendant in the form of a lion's head: greenish glass.

666—673. Small oval medallions of glass with designs impressed. *Nos. 667—673 from Spalato in Dalmatia.*

666. A ram: above it, two birds. Brilliantly iridescent.
667. Leda and the swan.
668. A boar.
669. Head of a bearded man wearing a wreath.
670. Subject effaced.
671. Head of Herakles, bearded, in the lion's scalp.
672. Head of man.
673. Bust of a man. Byzantine work.

674—728. *Terra-Cottas.*

The thousands of terra-cotta potsherds, which the Greeks required for ostracizing one another, came from the coarse jars of daily use, and not from the painted vases. There were wine jars always at hand: long cylindrical vessels with two handles and a pointed foot to fix in a deeply sanded floor: see no. 841. The wine jars made at Thasos, Cnidos and Rhodes always bore a stamp on one handle to certify their capacity: and for some reason these handles were generally broken off and preserved. There were also much larger vases, termed *pithoi*, intended for holding stores. These were large enough to serve as dwelling-places in case of need; or even from choice, as with Diogenes: and they were frequently used as coffins. The coffins of the Etruscans were generally of terra-cotta, but of more suitable form. These are large boxes with groups of figures in relief round the sides and a large reclining figure of the deceased on the top. And in modelling terra-cotta the Etruscans were renowned: so much so, that the earliest and most sacred statues in Rome were obtained from them: but probably they had themselves acquired the art from the Greeks. The Greeks of all ages delighted in terra-cotta statuettes, for ornamenting their houses, and for interment in tombs. Far the finest of these come from Tanagra in Bœotia, and date from between 400 and 300 B.C.: and most of them appear to be portraits. Such statuettes were generally made in moulds, the faces and the details of the drapery being finished off by hand afterwards: and there is always a square hole in the back to allow the dilated air to escape from the interior during the baking. The commoner sorts of these statuettes often represent deities; and particularly the deities of the nether world, the upper half of whose figures alone is modelled, as if they were rising out of the ground. Ears, eyes, and other parts of the body, were also modelled in terra-cotta for dedication at shrines as thankofferings for recovery from disease. Terra-cotta dolls with moveable limbs, and other toys, are sometimes found in children's graves. In the island of Melos and elsewhere in Greece some delicate terra-cotta reliefs have been found, which date from about 500 B.C. In these, the figures have been coloured: and the background has been cut away, so that the gilded woodwork, or other substance to which they were affixed, was seen between each figure. The ordinary terra-cotta reliefs were more in favour with the Romans than with the Greeks: and they must have formed the ordinary decorations in the terra-cotta city which became a city of marble under the rule of Augustus. The Roman terra-cotta lamps, dating from about 50 B.C. to 350 A.D. are of some interest: partly from the reliefs on them, and partly from the makers' names stamped underneath.

674—696. Terra-cotta statuettes, etc.

674. Head of a woman: a diadem above the hair. The back is not moulded. 8.

675. Head of a woman, with diadem and necklace. Broken off from a figure. 7½.

676. Figure of a woman from the waist upward. She wears a tall headdress in the front of which is an ear of corn: and has heavy drapery over her breast. The back is not moulded, but is ribbed like a leaf. 7¼. *From Sardinia.*

677. Bust of a woman wearing necklace and modius. 4¼. *From Catania.*

678. Part of similar bust. 3. *From Catania.*

679. Figure of a woman, fully robed. 3¼. *From Sicily.*

680, 681. Portions of similar figures. *From Sicily.*

682. Portion of similar figure. 4½. *From Veii.*

683. Figure of a woman, fully robed. 10.

684. Another. 7.

685—687. Heads of similar figures. *From Syracuse.*

688, 689. Female heads seen in profile, in low relief. 1½. *From Syracuse.*

690. Satyr's head, full face, in low relief. 1⅜. *From Syracuse.*

691. Female head, the neck ending in a point. 2¼.

692. Mask with formal curls and headdress. 2⅝.

693. Part of face from a figure. 3.

694. Eye. 2½.

695. Ear. 2.

696. Front part of foot wearing sandal. 2¾. 5.

697—717. Reliefs, in terra-cotta.

697. Amazon armed with axe defending herself from a griffin. Much broken. At the head of the panel is a leaf ornament. 7. 3½. *From Veii.*

698. Griffin trampling on a warrior. Much broken. 3⅛. 3. *From Veii.*

699. A young Satyr, kneeling on one knee and gathering grapes from a vine. 8. 5. *From Veii.*

700. A woman, fully draped. Much broken. 2¾. 3¼. *From Veii.*

701. Feet of a figure. An ornamental border below. 4½. 5½. *From Veii.*

702. A woman, winged, and fully robed, holding a lion by the paw. 6. 9.

703. Portion of four racing horses in a chariot. 6¾. 4½.

704. Portion of a female figure. 5½. 4½.

705. Portion of a youth, winged, and playing the double pipes. 3¼. 3.

706. A man kneeling and raising another man on his shoulder. 2⅛. 2¼.

707. A colonnade of four Corinthian columns; below it an arched basement and above it three large leaf ornaments. Between the columns, a fountain and two figures of a youth on pedestals. 11. 9½.

708. A woman, fully robed, standing under a portico. 3. 2¼. It is from some larger relief.

709. Another like it. 3¼. 2½.

710. Eagle with spread wings, standing on an acanthos plant. 3½. 2¾. It is from some larger object.

711. Gorgon's head, surrounded by conventional ornaments. 6. 6. From a building.

712—717. Architectural mouldings.

718—728. Lamps, in terra-cotta.

718. Relief of seated figure, half draped. Below, ΚΕΛϹΕΙ, Celsii (probably, Celsius Pompeius). *From Sicily.*

719. Ornamental pattern in relief. *From Sicily.*

720. In relief, head of Zeus seen above an eagle holding a thunderbolt in its claws.

721. In relief, combat of two gladiators. Below, C·OPPI·RES, *Caius Oppius Restitutus.*

722. In relief, comic and tragic mask. Below, CIVNBIT, *Caius Junius Bit...(?).*

723. In relief, a figure, robed. Below, CMAREV, *Caius Marius Euporus.*

724. In relief, a dog running.

725. In relief, a woman, winged and fully robed, carrying a palm-branch and a shield, on which are letters, HFSC (?). It has a triangular handle with a pattern in relief.

726. The upper part moulded in the form of a bull's head. The handle is crescent-shaped.

727. In relief, head of Zeus Ammon. Below, PASAVG, *Passienus* (?) *Augurinus* (?).

728. Lamp with tall foot, which bears in relief Athenê, seen in full face, fully robed and armed with helmet, shield, spear, the Ægis and the Gorgoneion. $6\frac{7}{8}$.

729—738. Marble.

729. Fragment of relief. A boy holding a scroll towards a bearded man, who also holds a scroll. 6. 5. *From Veii.*

730. Head of a bearded man, seen in full face. $5\frac{1}{2}$. $3\frac{1}{2}$. Part of a relief.

731. Piece of moulding in white marble. $3\frac{1}{2}$. $2\frac{1}{4}$. *From Palestrina.*

732. Another in giallo antico. $4\frac{1}{2}$. $1\frac{1}{2}$. *From the Villa of Munatius Plancus at Tivoli.*

733. Another in rosso antico. $3\frac{1}{2}$. $1\frac{1}{4}$. *From the Sette Sale (by the Baths of Titus) at Rome.*

734. Another in rosso antico. $2\frac{3}{4}$. $1\frac{1}{4}$. *From the Baths of Titus at Rome.*

735. Piece of Africano marble. 3. $1\frac{1}{8}$. *From Carthage.*

736. Fragment of the Lower Bema at Athens.

737. Fragment of the Upper Bema.

738. Piece of Pentelic marble from the Parthenon.

739—759. Building materials.

739—741. Pieces of Roman bricks from buildings on the Via Appia.

742. Piece of Roman brick, with part of potter's stamp, MBOF (?). *From Somersetshire.*

743. Piece of Roman brick. *From Somersetshire.*

744. Piece of Roman mortar. *From the walls of Silchester (Calleva Atrebatum).*

745, 746. Pieces of coloured stucco. *From the Baths of Caracalla at Rome.*

747, 748. Pieces of blue and of red colour.

749. Fragments of stucco. *From the Temple of Heracles at Girgenti.*

750. Iron cramp, with lead soldered to it. *From the Parthenon.*

751, 752. Small pieces of *From the Baths of Caracalla.*
753. mosaic pavement. *From the Baths of Titus.*

754, 755. Small stones from Of porphyry.
756, 757. mosaic pavement. Of serpentine.

758. Small piece of glass from a mosaic. *From the Baths of Caracalla.*

759. Eighteen small cubes of blue glass from a mosaic. *From Italica near Seville.*

760—775. Miscellaneous.

760. Vase of Egyptian porcelain, probably made at Naucratis, but found in Italy. 3½.

761. Alabastron of ivory. 3⅝. *From Veii.*

762. Writing tablet, of Etruscan black-ware. 7½. 3¼. Plain. *From Chiusi.*

763. Ivory die.

764. Tessera, inscribed COS IV DES. *False.*

765. Tessera, inscribed SC on one side and IV on the other. *Also false.*

766. Astragalos of bone. *From Corinth.*

767. Astragalos of glass.

768. Minute fragments of the lining of a chariot.

769. Byzantine weight of lead bearing the letters ογΛ in silver, i.e. οὐγκία α΄, one ounce.

770. A cylindrical object, narrowing toward the centre and bearing incised lines at each end. 2. Etruscan.

771, 772. Two conical whorls, each bearing nine lines incised in groups of three each.

773, 774. Two spherical whorls : plain.

775. String of fifteen carnelian beads, nearly elliptical, a carnelian scaraboid, and an onyx elliptical bead.

776—832. *Engraved Gems.*

Long before the Greeks began to engrave valuable stones for signets, the Egyptians had been engraving their scarabæi, and the Assyrians their cylinders which impressed designs as they were rolled over smooth surfaces. The Greeks never adopted the cylinder at all; and they only adopted the scarabæus in a modified form, the scaraboid, in which the details of the beetle's back were hardly indicated. But the Etruscans adopted the scarabæus readily : and between 600 and 300 B.C. they displayed great skill in producing gems in this form. The designs were generally borrowed from Greek works of other sorts: a butting bull, for example, from the coins of Thurium : see. nos. 777—780. The earliest gems found in Greek soil are shaped like beans (as are many of the earliest coins), and bear designs of plants and animals depicted in a heraldic style. They date from about 700 B.C., and are commonly called Island gems, as they are mostly found in the Greek islands. The ordinary gems of the Greeks and Romans were thin slices of stone, shewing a flat surface of oval form above and below : the finest dating from about 400 B.C. The subjects engraved are very varied: and the names of many engravers are known, partly from references in ancient writers, and partly from signatures on the gems themselves. It was fashionable in Rome to collect gems ; and many great collections were formed there from Cæsar's time onward : and this fashion caused gems to be manufactured there in large numbers ; for the most part, of little merit : see nos. 783—825. The worship of Mithras in the Roman Empire, and afterwards the Gnostic heresy are illustrated by large classes of gems, designed under their influence: and subsequently the art of gem engraving was continued in Persia under the Sassanian Monarchy: see nos. 826—829. The cutting of Cameos began about 300 B.C. and was thenceforth practised along with the old art of engraving: being especially used for portraits, which were first introduced on gems about the time of Alexander the Great: see nos. 830—832.

776. Chalcedony. A horse, grazing: above it, a crescent. *From Nineveh.*

777. Sard. (Etruscan scarabæus.) A three-horsed chariot, seen from the front.

778. Sard. (Etruscan scarabæus.) A stag, standing still: above it, the sun.

779. Sard. (Etruscan scarabæus.) A warrior, armed with helmet and shield and spear, kneeling on one knee.

780. Sard. (Etruscan scarabæus, the back cut down.) A bull, butting.

781. Pale sard. A horseman spearing a lion. *From Persia.*

782. Pale sard. A horseman with helmet and shield. *From Persia.*

783. Sard. Athenê, robed and armed with helmet and shield and spear. On her left hand stands Nikê: below it, a short column. *From Girgenti in Sicily.*

784. Green jasper. Perseus with Medusa's head. *From Egypt.*

785. Red jasper. Apollo with the lyre. *From Egypt.*

786. Red jasper. A warrior in full armour. *From Egypt.*

787. Red jasper, or paste. Nemesis with the wheel and the scales. *From Egypt.*

788. Banded sard. Harpocrates. *From Thebes in Egypt.*

789. Red jasper. Apollo with the bow. *From Spalato in Dalmatia.*

790. Red jasper. Athenê. *From Spalato.*

791. Sard. Athenê, with her spear across her shoulder, running. *From Spalato.*

792. Opaque sard. Athenê. *From Spalato.*

793. Sard. Athenê : beside her, the word ΛΛΑжΙΛΛ. *From Spalatô.*

794. Onyx. Heracles. *From Spalato.*

795. Sard. Hermes, standing by a column. *From Spalato.*

796. Onyx. A warrior, seated, with his shield beside him, and resting his head on his hand. *From Spalato.*

797. Yellow jasper. A woman dancing. *From Spalato.*

798. Red jasper. A woman raising some object in her hands. *From Spalato.*

799. Pale sard. A huntsman; carrying two hares in his hands, and at the end of a pole over his shoulder a basket on which a quail is seated. *From Spalato.*

800. Pale sard. A woman, holding a flower and a rake. *From Spalato.*

801. Serpentine. A man, holding a flower and a rake. *From Spalato.*

802. Yellow jasper. A warrior before a statue of Athenê : at the sides, the letters H and I. *From Spalato.*

803. Red jasper. A warrior fastening his greaves, Erôs looking on. *From Spalato.*

804. Sard. Two figures dancing. *From Spalato.*

805. Onyx. A man holding a prancing horse. *From Spalato.*

806. Sard. A winged figure riding a horse and leading another by its side. *From Spalato.*

807. Sardonyx. Inscribed ΧΑΙΡΕ ΤΥΧΗ. *From Spalato.*

808. Sard. A dolphin. *From Spalato.*

809. Onyx. A dolphin. *From Spalato.*

810. Agate. A rabbit. *From Spalato.*

811. Sard. An ant. *From Spalato.*

812. Burnt onyx. A crab. *From Spalato.*

813. Red jasper. A cock. *From Spalato.*

814. Onyx. A cock. *From Spalato.*

815. Sard : part of the setting in an iron ring remaining. A vase of the form termed *crater*, and beside it a cock. *From Salona in Dalmatia.*

816. Sard. A quail on a pillar. *From Spalato.*

817. Banded onyx. A horse, grazing : above it, an eagle. *From Spalato.*

818. Sard. An eagle on an altar : beside it two helmets with stars and a caduceus : i.e. emblems of Zeus, the Dioscuri and Hermes. *From Spalato.*

819. Pale sard. Emblems. *From Spalato.*

820. Sard. A woman's head in profile. *From Spalato.*

821. Sard. Bust of Athené in profile. *From Spalato.*

822. Red jasper. Erôs riding in a car drawn by a pair of doves. *From Spalato.*

823. Red jasper. Two Erotes climbing two ladders placed against a tree and throwing down fruit to two other Erotes who stand below. *From Verlika in Dalmatia.*

824. Sard : mounted in a modern ring. A man standing beneath a tree into the branches of which he is thrusting a long pole. *From Egypt.*

825. Sard : mounted in a modern ring. Three figures standing side by side : Asclepios and perhaps Hermes and Artemis. *From Samos.*

826. Sard : mounted in a modern seal. Mithras sacrificing a bull : around him, Mithraic emblems. Not ancient : probably made in the last century.

827. Limestone (?). A man in heavy vestments with uplifted arms : letters (apparently Greek) around. Probably Gnostic. *From Girgenti in Sicily.*

828. Sard. A man, wearing a Persian crown, riding in a four-horsed chariot. Probably Sassanian. *From Spalato.*

829. Sard. Bust of a bearded man wearing a Sassanian headdress, in profile. Inscription in Pehlvi characters around. *From Spalato.*

830. Cameo. A woman's head, slightly thrown back, in profile. *From Spalato.*

831. Cameo. Bust of Cleopatra with the asp. *From Spalato.*

832. Cameo. Two lions bearing a shrine on which three deities recline, one wearing the crown of Upper and Lower Egypt. *From Egypt.*

833. Bronze support of a casket in the form of the fore-part of a human-headed beast. *From Nineveh.*

834. Fragment of gold-leaf from the coating of an ivory. *From Nineveh.*

835. Gold ring with Sanskrit inscription reading, "·O Rāma, conquer!" *From India.*

श्री राम ज[य]
·· राम जय
जय राम

THE FOLLOWING ANTIQUITIES HAVE SINCE BEEN PRE-SENTED TO HARROW SCHOOL.

836—841. *By Captain Erskine Tudor Risk.* 1878.

836. A piece of white marble sculptured in relief with the head of a youth and the right hand raised to it, part of a larger subject. Roman work. *From Halicarnassos.*

837—840. Four pieces of white marble sculptured with portions of Greek architectural mouldings. *From Hali-carnassos.*

841. A large Rhodian wine jar; the pointed base broken off, and also the handle which would have borne the stamp. *From Halicarnassos.*

842—850. *By Mr Greville John Chester.* 1886.

842—846. Five small terra-cotta masks in very low relief with faint traces of colour, three of Medusa and two of a bearded satyr. *From Capua.*

847. A terra-cotta weight with a figure of a bird in relief. *From Tarentum.*

848. Rough terra-cotta mask. *From South Italy.*

849. Disk with head of a river god in relief. *From South Italy.*

850. Glass bottle, brilliantly iridescent. *From Tyre.*

CAMBRIDGE: PRINTED BY C. J. CLAY, M.A. AND SONS, AT THE UNIVERSITY PRESS.

Lightning Source UK Ltd.
Milton Keynes UK
UKHW020632170822
407432UK00006B/945